LEADERSHIP SKILLS

MOHAN R. KHANVILKAR.

INDIA • SINGAPORE • MALAYSIA

ISBN
Paperback 979-8-89673-840-4
Hardcase 979-8-89744-554-7

This book is dedicated to my father Late
Shri. Raghunathrao Gangaramrao Khanvilkar
who always worked for helping the people around
and always remained as an institution for telling
importance of *sincerity*, *honesty*, and *hard working*
in people's wellbeing activities.

Thanks to Editors:

Madhukar Phal

and

M/s Notion Press Media Pvt. Ltd.

Contents

Preface ... *ix*

Foreword ... *xi*

Introduction ... *xiv*

1. Leader ... 1
2. Improve Positive Power ... 4
3. Working Style ... 7
4. Rely On Individuality ... 11
5. Develop Self-Awareness ... 14
6. Personality Development ... 17
7. Self-Confidence ... 21
8. Guru Within You ... 24
9. Leading By Vision ... 27
10. Managing Discipline ... 30

11. Power Of Coolness 34

12. Improve Honesty. 37

13. Concept Of Perfection 40

14. Self-Development 43

15. Managing Self 47

16. Spiritual Approach 51

17. Importance Of Honesty 55

18. Knowing About Oneness 59

19. Improve Will Power. 62

20. Work As A Play. 67

21. Awareness Of Thoughts 70

22. Never Be Invincible 73

23. A Good Listener. 77

24. Significance Of Spirituality 80

25. Build High Performance 83

26. Culture Of Team Spirit. 87

27. Stress Management 91

28. Quality Of Work Life 96

29. Potential Appraisal 99

30. Implement 'Kaizen' 101
31. Develop Human Relations 105
32. Importance Of Character 109
33. Functions Of A Leader. 113
34. Mind Management 117
35. A Successful Leader. 121
36. Leadership 124
37. Leader Is Mentor. 130
38. Developing Supervisory Skills. 133

About the Author 136

Supplementary Reading 138

PREFACE

The word 'Leader' is more popular in the business circles of the present corporate world. But in real sense, a very few people knows its meaning in right perceptive.

We all very well aware about the one fact that every individual has to do the work activities for producing goods and services that necessary for wellbeing of the human life. It is also known fact that such work activities are required to be done by an individual person for himself or by an individual being in capacity as a manager, officer, supervisor or a leader of any business organization for the purpose of getting the work activities done from other people.

While doing the work by a person for getting the work done from others it is essentially required by such person to possess the knowledge, skill, and a proper behaviour on basis of which he will be able to guide, motivate and inspire those people to do the work activities enthusiastically with zeal. This is also required to be possessed by an individual who do work activities for him.

I had an opportunity to work with the superiors, leaders, and even owners of different organizations in the industries. While working as a Human Resources Management personnel with them, I have keenly observed their leadership styles.

My prime objective behind writing this book on “Leadership” is to provide its readers the basis of knowledge, skills that I have with me by virtue of my forty-one years of work experiences in seven different industrial organizations. I am sure this book will be very much useful to the Leaders working in any capacity for different industrial organization.

I am thankful to the entire team members and family members who supported me by extending cooperation while writing this book till the last moments of its completion.

&&&

FOREWORD

Leadership is a skill that motivates groups of people to act to accomplish a common objective. It is a process of inspiring, guiding and helping others to work enthusiastically towards achievement of objectives. Leadership is essential because it establishes a clear vision and communicates effectively with its subordinates and colleagues. Organizational leadership defines haw decisions are made, teams are motivated and objectives are achieved within an organization be it a company or an institution. It plays a fundamental role in shaping an entity's culture, productivity and overall success. It is very difficult to simplify it for all the concerned to understand it so as to practice it objectively. Mr. Mohan Khanvilkar took the challenge and came out with this modestly sized book titled as "LEADERSHIP SKILLS". He had studied the leadership aspects from all possible perspectives and came out with this work classified in specific issues coming across the process of leading a team in an organization aiming at a specified goal. His articulation in each of the chapters makes the theme quite clear. A special reference may be made to the focus, though in brief yet very clear on self-awareness of divine power from Vedanta theory.

Of course he could do justice to the task taken up also because of his long standing experience in the industrial field dealing with numerous combinations of work force and every time leading them to a successful achievement of the set goals and at the same time studding the behaviour of various leaders and sub-leaders impacting in the industrial scenario.

The chapters are all clearly structured and clearly expressed and easy to understand. He argues lucidly and persuasively making the reading of the work not only interesting but also thought provoking in the behavioral aspects of an organizations.

I felt privileged to pen down my impression on reading this work which will be a useful guide to the emerging leaders in the business circles.

Congratulations to Mr. Mohan Khanvilkar for such a impacting work in the field of organizational developments and wish him all the best for providing more such contributions in days to come.

Dr. Sharad Sawant

Director (Retd.)

Maharashtra Institute of Labour Studies,

Mumbai.

&&&

INTRODUCTION

I am knowing Mr. Mohan Raghunath Khanvilkar since -1985 when we met in Narmada Cement Company Ltd., at their Head Office in Mumbai. I am proud of the opportunity that I had to interact with him closely while he was working in Human Resources Department of Narmada cement.

I have seen and also experienced to some extent the leadership quality of Mr. Khanvilkar when he was managing the task of employee discipline in Narmada cement. I would say, he was a popular person during those days for managing employee discipline.

In addition to the Post-Graduation in HR Management education, he is having LL.B. degree. Initially, before joining in Narmada Cement, he worked in a Govt. of India Organization for about twelve years in different positions and gained work experience of accounts, contracts and labor departments.

After living Narmada Cement, he joined in a reputed infrastructure company i.e **AFCONS,** and thereafter he worked for many other companies which were also well known in doing infrastructure projects of construction industry.

I feel honored about the opportunity that have been given to me for introducing Mr. Khanvilkar the author of this book on **LEADERSHIP SKILLS**. I am also very much thankful to Mr. Khanvilkar for choosing this particular subject for this book which was desired by many leaders functioning in the organizations of industries like a political, business and social. In his book on 'Leadership Skills' he mentioned certain guiding principles and gave advice to the leaders which is most useful to them for becoming a successful leader. He tried to build a Leader with all sorts of good qualities and capacities that essentially required by a person who want to be a successfully a great leader. In the definition of the word 'Leader' he considered that every person in this world doing any kind of good work activity that necessary for producing goods and services is a Leader.

Further to this, he mentioned that the person representing the organization in his capacity as a Manager or In-Charge of an organization in any field industry is a Leader.

He has also said that even a person in his individual capacity does the work activities for himself without representing to any organization is also a Leader.

While advising on the 'Leadership Skill' development, he emphasized on the awareness of 'self' which is a divine power consciousness existing within every individual human being.

Vinayak S. Golivadekar

B. Sc. (Hons.), M. B. A.

ൠൠൠ

1. LEADER

1. Why Leader is necessary?

Every human individual born on this planet is required to do various activities that are necessary to produce goods and services essentially needed for the wellbeing, survival, of the entire human community and to enjoy better quality of life in the present world. Such activities may be for and in relation to industrial or business organization, or in relation to any political, social and even spiritual organizations. The work activities that are necessary to be done by an individual personally without having any relation with any kind of organization also come under this category. While understanding the concept of any human activity in the context of leadership, it is needless to mention that a person or persons performing such work activities must possess knowledge, skill, and adequate experience of the subject of those activities. Even if the people who do not have the knowledge, skill and experience, may go ahead with work activities but success in those activities will be very limited.

However, if he/she is provided with appropriate guidance and directions by a proper knowledgeable person in relation to the work activities, he/she may perform well and do the work activities more effectively, efficiently and can produce good results for the organization and even for himself.

Now, it is most relevant for me to answer the question i.e. who is the proper knowledgeable person to lead and guide the people appropriately to perform their work activities. My answer to this particular question is 'LEADER'.

'Leader' can be seen in a business scenario in different names, forms, designations and positions. For example, in an industrial, business or in any organization an individual is given designation to his position as a Manager, in a political field organization he/she may be named as a Leader or **Netaji** *and in professional field* *may be in position as a Doctor, Lawyer, C.A. or Malik.* But, his/her duty and prime objective of being there will be common i.e. to influence, and to inspire people with him by providing the proper knowledge, and guidance to do the work willingly and efficiently.

@@@

2. Improve Positive Power

Organization, be it an industrial, business or any other, it's most important function is to produce goods and services that are ultimately necessary for well-being of the people. For achieving this objective, obviously those work activities have to be performed by the employees and the person who is inspiring, influencing people to do the work as per the necessity. The person inspiring, influencing is a manager/supervisor or a Leader at work place.

We are already aware of the fact that, getting requisite human response from the employees at work is a challenging job for a manager. This is in spite of him being an authority to take any disciplinary action against an employee who is reluctant to do his work. But, in such a situation the Manager being a Leader of human beings needs to be aware about the very important fact that, he is already filled with great and intense powers in his position as a Manager itself.

'Vedanta' philosophy, the science of consciousness told us that every individual human being in this world is a divine soul i.e. Atman and it is already filled with a great and intense powers within itself. Only thing he or she need to do is to utilize that intense power gifted by God within himself/herself at appropriate Time.

The Leader of any organization facing any difficult situation for getting the willing response from his followers to do the work activities, must deeply look into within his heart to find out the real solution to the problem instead of searching and depending upon the remedy outside.

The Leader, who is sharing positive power with his followers, must be aware of the fact that he is not sharing the power of a Manager's position in the organization, but his personal power that he possesses as a gift given to him by the God itself. In order to build faith, trust and confidence between himself and followers, he is also required to share the resources, responsibility and necessary authority with his followers.

Also, he /she must remove the obstacles, difficulties coming in the path of the employees, followers while performing duties at the work place in the organization.

@@@

3. Working Style

We have *discussed enough about the necessity of a leader for any kind of organizational functioning to produce best quality goods and services those are essential for survival and well-being of people living in human communities in the present world. If we look at the past histories of our nation or historical background of many countries of the world, we learn very well that many miracles, victories, and even wonders were happened in the world only because of and due to the outstanding leadership qualities of eminent personalities like Chhatrapati Shivaji Maharaja, Maharana Pratap, Zashiki Rani Lakshmibai, Mahatma Gandhi,* Swami Viveka Nanda of our nation and many great leaders in of the world.

Sometimes, we learn that the Leaders are born and not made. But, personally, speaking, I agree with this concept to some extent. Because, the leader and his leadership is a basic necessity of the entire business community of the present world. It is true that the present world has enough human talent and intelligence.

But, unless and until employees have been provided with a proper guidance by a leader having thorough knowledge of the subject, and work activities, employees will find many difficulties to go ahead effectively and concequently results will be unsatisfactory. The Leader, who is required to do his work of leadership for activating the work effectively, efficiently and successfully in any organization, must acquire various good qualities in regard to the knowledge, personal character, physical and mental health. Also, he needs to adopt an appropriate style of work for an effective Leadership.

> **Leadership styles** *means a pattern of behavior which a leader adopts himself for influencing behavior of his team members or followers to do their work activities efficiently. There are three different styles of leadership:* **(a)** *Empowering i.e. democratic style involving the subordinates,* **(b)** *Power style, i.e. autocratic and democratic.*

(c) *Orientation Styles – employee oriented and task oriented.*

While learning about the above stated three different styles of leadership, we have seen that no one particular style is operative at all places in the organization.

A Leader, without any rigidity should try to get the desired results as the situation warrants. Sometimes, a leader need to motivate his people through rewards and other positive actions. But wherever necessary a leader should also take negative actions against the erring employees if the situation so warrants.

Leadership starts within the leader itself. It continues when the leader can assess where the people are and then proceed with the step-by-step movement of the people towards the fulfillment of his vision.

EMPOWERING LEADER*: It is an ideal form of leadership. Because the empowering leader builds relationships with his people, communicates positive vision,* and motivates them to achieve results. The leader equips followers to produce results as per his choice.

A true leader is a partner with his people in success. Therefore, in the present circumstances, a leader should follow the democratic style by involving subordinates in the decision-making process.

ஐஐஐ

4. Rely On Individuality

Leader should always function on basis of his own individual power that is already existing within him. Because, the principle of spiritual science said that every human being in this world is in reality a bliss-filled soul. Hence, the Leader need to realize that his true nature is the power of his soul i.e. 'Atman' within him. Hence, the leader should always listen to the instructions that coming for him from within that being a real pure consciousness.

The most important function of a leader is inspiring and influencing his followers to do whatever he directs them to do towards accomplishment of the goals. If a leader wanted to influence and inspire his followers and the people around him, he should keep away his ego state of mind. He needs to be aware about the flow of a inner light of his real being inside within himself which is a great pure energy that makes true relationship between him and his followers.

Leader must also realize that every human being has a divine power within, which helps him/her understand the energy of others. This is as per a very fundamental principle of Indian spiritual science i.e. Vedanta philosophy.

In the present world, we normally observe that, in most of the organizations either it is industrial, business or political organization; their Leaders do their act of functioning on basis of their ego state of mind ignoring the fact of their true nature i.e. quality of individual power existing within them all the time. The leader when he identifies himself on basis of his ego and starts functioning on basis of it, his mind knowingly or unknowingly creates a lot of confusions in the minds of his followers. This situation of confusion immediately occurs at shop floor of the work place. Because of such kind of acts by the leader, his functions do not come out of his real nature and awareness which is self-realization.

The real art of positive leadership is to do work beyond the boundaries of the Ego that is between the leader's outward action and the power of self- i.e. Atman.

'Vedanta philosophy' a science of Indian spirituality says that the real illness is the illness of Ego. Because, the very basis of ego state of mind is the outcome of facts gathered in mind from outside information and not from the knowledge that the leader has out of his 'self-realization.' Therefore, leader must do his functions to influence his followers essentially at such a place where he can be true to his own being. He can use his individualism a power within him which is free from Ego.

In this respect the great leader of spiritual science "Swami Vivekananda" used to say that only immature people act out of ego. Truly mature persons do their act of leading others only out of completeness and totality of their own individual qualities that are entirely on basis of spiritual wisdom of Vedanta. Swami Vivekananda's teaching also tell us that instead of being led by a sense of ego state of mind, bring your own intelligence and walk alone to have courage. He used to say that essentially each human being has an individual divinity within him i.e. Atman.

@@@

5. Develop Self-Awareness

In the present world, every individual human being is a leader of his own cause of action while doing the work in any position with own capacity. The working field may be professional, business organization or it can be political or any other kind of organization. The very essential thing for every such individual person is that he should ask himself one basic question i.e**. who am I?** And answer to this question is I am an **Atman**. It means a '**Soul**' that stays within every human body and it is a part of being pure consciousness which is a 'self-awareness'.

When we talk about the 'self- awareness' of each individual person, it means knowing about the power of consciousness of his own which is within the body of an individual at spiritual level. In this regard a message of the Bhagwat Geeta tells us that, it is a 'SELF' [Atmagyan] an energy to create an excellence in whatever act an individual person performs, whether it is in capacity as a warrior, a leader including a leader of his own profession.

For achieving good excellent results in leadership, the attribute of true self-confidence is most fundamental thing which is born of deep self-awareness.

The Leader, means a person who is required to give first priority to 'self-awareness' while leading to and begins his functions.

However, in today's world of leadership, unfortunately the leaders are very rarely functioning on basis of their self-awareness. Instead of functioning on basis of 'self-awareness' most of the time we have seen that many leaders are operating themselves on basis of their falls identification which is the ego state of mind that mainly on basis of the information they gained from the data of the physical world.

Leaders who worked with Self-awareness are always in totality of secret power of self-confidence, courage and energy within themselves. The leaders who worked on basis of such self-awareness are now known as great leaders, great warriors as they have proved themselves as successful leaders in true sense.

The 'Bhagwat Geeta' which is the essence of Vedanta philosophy taught us that the 'Swadharm' the identity or the 'dignity' of our self-nature if we forget, then we also move away from the real meaning of our life. Therefore, the leader if he leads his followers without knowing his real identity which is 'self-awareness' of true being, i.e. pure consciousness, then he cannot be a successful leader.

Intrinsic and mystic self-power is only a real power and if it is missing, the whole life of an individual becomes confusing. Therefore, it is said that one should build his house on the rock of 'self-awareness', so that the life will be living a truly fulfilling life to become a leader of the team succefully.

A Leader should always focus internally, awakening his consciousness which is the secret of charismatic and highly effective leadership. A great leader is a person who activates his deeper levels of consciousness and does things with passion to get the excellence in results.

ꝶꝶꝶ

6. Personality Development

Leader's prime duty is to influence and inspire his people around to do whatever he wanted to do towards the achievement of his pre-determined goals and accomplishment of his vision.

A manager of a particular organization can take any disciplinary action against an employee who commits misconduct. But, the leader without having any authority or power of his chair position, will be unable to take any action against his employee for not listening to the instructions given to him. The Leader possesses only personal power which he gets from his own personality traits on basis of which he has to impress, influence, and inspire his followers to do the work activities with necessary cooperation from others. Therefore, every leader needs to put his efforts consistently in developing personality attributes which are mentioned here below:

a) **Self-Confidence**: self- confidence, courage and strength is required with a Leader in order to enable him to function as an effective leader.

He can acquire his confidence and can get courage if he is thorough with the knowledge, skill in regard to the subject that he has to deal with and a proper behavior towards his followers for getting the work done. He also needs to possess a good sound health status, enough strength, and a proper attitude that will enable him to guide his followers appropriately. Every human being must be aware of the fact, and should believe that either he or she, by nature itself is a person with courage, confident, and strength.

b) **Communication:** Every leader must be essentially a good communicator. A leader should be always with a Good communication skill that necessary for becoming a great successful leader in his field or any other field of his choice. His success as a leader will be in danger if he does not possess a good communication skill. A good communicator also essentially required to be a good listener. If he is lacking this particular quality of his personality, then he will not be able to function as a good leader.

Therefore, a leader must develop his skill of listening to the others.

c) **Good Learner:** A leader should develop his habit of learning especially from his day to day work activities. He should never mind to learn from his followers, subordinates and his employees. His learning habits will always help to enhance his knowledge that necessary for him to become a good leader.

d) **Developing a Vision:** Every leader must be a visionary person. Without a vision a person cannot be considered to be a leader. A person without a vision is like a driver of a vehicle driving without knowing his destination. A visionary leader is one who always wants to see something new which is beyond the boundaries of his thoughts jurisdiction. The 'Vedanta' philosophy says that the ultimate i.e. Brahman is in existence inherently within each human being. Therefore, a leader has to share his vision in life of others so that he can automatically move towards stronger position of a leader.

In addition to the development of above said four important attributes of a personality, a leader should also develop many other qualities of his personality such as a mutual trust, confidence, Self-awareness, Innovation, and Passion. Improvement in these qualities will bring him to a particular standard that ultimately will help him to get the confidence of his followers.

@@@

7. Self-Confidence

A leader means an invisible message constantly coming from a person performing a role of the Leadership and this message is for his people around. This real message is coming from actions and activities of a leader and it is from his spiritual heart. When we do our work activities spontaneously with an awareness of consciousness within, we find joyfulness in work that we perform and the same makes us playful at the moment in our actions. It is a Message coming from the mystical within ourselves showing a quality of our real being itself and it is naturally cheerful and joyful commanding trust and confidence of people around while functioning as a leader.

When a leader is in natural, spontaneous mode of mind, a person whoever comes in his contact, confidently attracted to his leadership quality. But, in today's real world we hardly find such kind of quality in a leader. Instead, most of the places we find the faces of leaders with a lot of stress, tension, and anxiety.

Because of such condition of their mind, the people around them are confused with a lots of doubts and consequently they are unable to be confident about their leader. Every leader should spend some time in asking a question to himself as to **Who am** I? He will get the answer to his question that he is neither his body nor mind but he is a real being i.e. **Atman.** For knowing this truth of real being within him, he required to make his mind completely clear by removing all unwanted thoughts unnecessarily crowded in mind, so as to get mind free from all sorts of distractions. Thereafter, he needs to think deeply to get complete peace of mind after realization that his real being is 'Atman' which is a part of consciousness. His functioning begins shining with the power of spiritual heart and reflection of functional activities seen through mind which will be automatically influencing people around in getting confidence of the leader. This is given in spiritual science i.e. 'Bhagavad Geeta' told by Lord Krishna to Arjun.

A leader is required to be aware of the power of his Atman, real being consciousness that brings the quality in the Leadership roles which will ultimately give confidence to the people around the Leader.

@@@

8. Guru Within You

Leadership is for influencing people to do various kinds of work activities that essentially necessary to produce goods and services for wellbeing of human life on this planet. In most of the situations, we see that many people have misunderstanding about the correct meaning or interpretation of the word leader and the concept behind the same. A common man understanding about a leader means a person who leads people only in political field. Whereas in addition to the political field, learned people's understanding is leader means a person who is in the position of a manager or at higher position in business or industrial organization or even in any other organization of any field in position as a manager or a leader for getting the work activities done from the employees. But in addition to these interpretations about the leadership and leader, we need to understand that the leadership is also necessary for an individual in the activities done by him for wellbeing of his own cause and others. Hence, every individual either he or she, essentially required to be a Leader when he does any kind of work activities.

Eventually the 'guru' is simply a word or a device to remind us that we need to listen to the voice of our own 'Atman.' We should realize that there is a guide residing within us which is 'Atman' and we must listen to the voice of it. Make yourself less important to the 'Ego' and listen to the guide inside, that is 'Atman'. This guide will lead you as a real master in leadership. The highest human virtues of courage, energy and confidence live within the human consciousness being inside and that is the guide and real guru.

A Leader being a 'guru' of himself is a word of spirituality. We must be aware that each of us is having capacity of becoming a 'Guru' of ourselves. It is true that our technical skill, knowledge and experiences are a part of leadership intelligence. But we need to also remember that there is a power of spiritual strength within us that make us dynamic with full bright inner light illuminating charisma that touches to every aspect of work.

®®®

9. Leading By Vision

In many situations, we see that the leaders of the people of any business, political or industrial organizations lead the people on basis of fear. While doing their activities in position as a leader, they use the tactics of making people afraid of some kind of pain or they offer them some rewards. We also learn from the history that the 'reward' and 'punishment' have worked as the 'carrot' and 'stick'. The carrot tempts on one hand with some reward and on the other hand the stick is always to beat people in some manner or the other. However, one thing is clear that such kind of leadership action is not in accordance with or on basis of the vision.

People wanted to know and to watch something new from the action of their leader which will be beyond the reach of their thinking. The leadership is all about influencing and inspiring the people.

Leader is required to see something new which will be beyond the reach of his follower's thoughts and therefore it will motivate followers.

Hence, leader needs to do something extraordinary that will encourage his followers and others through the nobleness of his vision. The leader has to function keeping in view that his people will be inspired, energized with positivity. Leader should function with possibility of reaching to the peak of his own potentials so that his entire energy is devoted to the higher cause.

Alexander the Great was the Leader with an extraordinary vision. He had the ability to make his Army believe that he was unifying the world. Leadership is all about to motivate, inspire and encourage people through the nobleness of vision. Leader needs to remember that the Fear and Greed create trouble in people's mind as they are tools of the neurotic leader. Lord Buddha's key principle of his social vision was revolutionary religion which was not depending upon 'Fear' or 'Greed'. His religion was on basis of self-realization. Buddha emphasized vision of self-realization that means motivations are based upon something higher which is vision.

Lord Buddha's philosophy of spirituality made it clear that the great leaders have not made only the better world outside themselves in whatever capacity they had, but also they made a better world within themselves.

ઢઢઢ

10. Managing Discipline

The success of every progressive organization depends upon a proper behavior of the employees at work. The right kind of attitude of employees and their leader is an essential quality that produces a proper behavior of the employees at work. The right kind of attitude and behavior of the employees at work basically comes by observing the rules of discipline. Therefore, it is said that, the discipline is backbone of every organization doing either industrial or any other business activity. Hence, while doing the activities in business and even industrial organization, every leader must teach to his followers and employees to follow the rules of discipline very strictly.

Because of some statutory restrictions, employer or any leader of the employees has very limited scope at his disposal to exercise his rights of administering rules of discipline. Hence, while maintaining discipline of an organization, every employer is always guided by the principles of natural justice, directions and rulings given by the Honorable Supreme Court of our nation in various judgments.

The procedure of dealing with and initiating disciplinary action against an employee who committed misconduct is given to some extent in the Industrial Employment Standing Orders Act. 1946. Whenever an employee is to be awarded with punishment for the misconduct that is committed at work place, the employer is under legal obligation to initiate disciplinary action by conducting a domestic enquiry against employee who has committed misconduct. There is no a complete codified law so far available on basis of which the employer can take disciplinary action except principles of natural justice.

Two important Principles of Natural Justice are: (a) No man shall be punished unheard. (b) No man shall be judge of his own case.

The Supreme Court gave certain guidelines in this respect in various judgments which are as following:

- Allow the delinquent employee to deny his guilt and establish innocence. This is to be done only when he is told about the charges of misconduct leveled against him.

- Give opportunity to the delinquent employee to defend himself by cross examining his witness in support of charges leveled.

- The enquiry against the employee should be fair and should be conducted by an impartial person.

- Punishment awarded should be in proportion with the misconduct committed.

IMPROVING ORGANISATION CULTURE:

The culture of an organization and meaningful relations between the management and employees has a crucial role in maintaining discipline in industrial organization. Discipline is a product of culture that an organization possesses at different levels of employee behavior, conduct and employee commitments towards organization. To have a right kind of environment and culture of discipline in an organization, the management has to identify the training needs of each employee at different places of the organization and implement Employee Training program me on regular basis.

Good human relations among employees, management and even leaders are most important. Therefore the Leader should understand such relations essentially in right perceptive and the differences if any needs to be sorted out immediately. This will help to have cordial industrial relations and harmony at work place. Similarly, every leader must develop the skills of interpersonal relations by having insight into the basic needs of the employees and the people around. For this purpose, he should be an able person to manage every individual employee's identity, recognition, and importance. These things will be possible for a leader if he becomes successful in building a mutual trust, confidence and faith between management and employees.

Also all the Leaders in industrial/business organizations need to understand and believe that the money spent by the organizations on its Employee Training and Development activities is an investment and not expenditure.

@@@

11. Power Of Coolness

We all live on this earth as a Leader of human being to some extent in public life and also in our own personal life. Most of the time we observe the situation amongst people and even with leaders who struggle with a disturbed kind of behavior pattern which they adopt for achieving success in their work activities as a leader.

Every individual person needs to keep in mind a simple principle that the work activities related to any kind of business, industry, political field, or in the field of sports, those activities must be performed with a calm, cool and peaceful mind. This message specially applies to a Leader whose duty is to inspire his people to follow him to do the various kinds of work activities. Most of the time, many leaders are having assumptions in their mind that if they shout at the employees or become aggressive in their style of work, they will be more effective in getting results in their duty as a leader. But in real sense it is not so. It is a wrong understanding on their part for the reason that if they are aggressive in their style of leadership there is a possibility of they becoming angry with the people at work and as a result of such anger situation the Leader may lose his confidence in thoughts and memory which may lead him to the condition of any kind of disaster at work place.

This principle of leadership applies in any field of activities. It can be seen in the world of business, it is seen in the world of politics and even in the world of sports and even religious activities. Look at the most successful sport person and Bharat Ratna award winner Sachin Tendulkar. He is the master of the cricket, whom we have always seen calm, cool, confident and assertive while playing cricket. Those leaders who are cool, always remembered as great leaders. When we try to understand the Aikido martial art of Japan, or the Judo martial art which is inspired by Buddha's principles of excellence in all spheres of life, we see that the martial artist uses the other person's energy very coolly to overthrow and defeat that other person. Hence, if we are attacked by the opponent person, we simply require to utilize with cool mind that man's energy and by combining it with our own energy, we will be the winner.

Lord Buddha used to say that the real miracles are residing in our own consciousness and to tap into these miracles we required to be a cool and with silent mind. According to Buddha's philosophy of spirituality, all actions which are born out of coolness of mind or out of meditative state of mind have a great power. Every human being has the capacity to function out of a state of inner coolness. Gautama Buddha taught us this technique of attaining inner coolness by telling us to watch our own breath. This technique was also told by Lord Shiva to Parvati. Therefore, the very important thing to achieve success is a peace and calmness in mind by watching our own breath. Whatever may be the situation or circumstances in the outside world, every leader must resolve by having a coolness in mind so as to enable him to remain undisturbed in his inside body which will help him to be aware of the real being i.e. Atman.

ଥଥଥ

12. Improve Honesty

While understanding the concept of leadership and the role of a leader in various kinds of institutions, organizations of public life, the word 'honesty' is considered more relevant. Because, honesty is also one important attribute of a leader's good character. It is said that if a leader's personality is without a good moral character with honesty, integrity, dignity and sincerity, then such a leader is like a building constructed without steel, cement, stones and sand which can collapse at any moment of time.

The children learn and pick up the real meaning of the term 'Honesty' in school at their early age. The principles of honesty are being taught to the children even at home by their parents. But in public life, in organizations of any business or professions it is unfortunate to see that the importance of honesty have been ignored knowingly or unknowingly. As a result of such ignorance, we see many incidents of scams, corruptions and even crimes. The issue of corruptions has come up in the politics to such a extent that the economy of the nation and even world itself is being affected very badly. Today, we observe that most of the organizations including political organizations and even individuals functioning in any field are busy in attainments of higher economic growth on basis of their dishonest behavior in business activities.

The Leader when he adopts a vision for improving and developing his organization, he needs to give more importance to the honesty of his own cause of activities and acts of his followers. In his functions as a leader, he is required to educate himself and his followers to do their works activities observing the essential aspects of honesty.

The honesty that exists within every human being is the value of an individual person. But in the present systems of overall business scenarios, including political field the status of honesty day by day is being polluted and detoriated because of the dishonest behavior of the leaders and their followers. Hence, the value of honesty is being disappeared in every walk of life.

Honesty cannot be built in minds of the people by making laws in the parliament. The only remedy to overcome the situation is to educate the leaders, their followers and even the people at all level through actions of the leaders working in any organization at all levels. The organizations should provide need base training inputs to the leaders and to the employees at all levels, so as to bring awareness among the employees about the importance of honesty.

We also need to believe that the quality of honesty can be nurtured, developed and improved at any stage of human life.

@@@

13. Concept Of Perfection

When a student appearing for an examination of any subject of his own choice is failed or didn't get success to as per his expectations, then he feels nervous. But, in accordance with the principle of spiritual science a Vedanta philosophy, such kind of thinking is incorrect. 'Vedanta' teaches us that the life is not about being faultless, but it is simply about knowing ourselves spiritually. Swami Vivekananda's teachings also tell us that the education is simply manifestation of perfection which is already within us. Vedanta teaches us that one should not be nervous, or blame himself even if he or she is failed in any examination. Similar thing is about a leader also. The Leader need not be restless even if he makes mistakes as a leader. He or she shouldn't think that all the time they will be winners. On the contrary what a leader needs to do is to learn more and improve more which is the right path to move forward with his followers courageously in life of leadership roles.

Leadership should begin fearlessly without a fear of making any mistakes or fault. The leader needs to remember that his real life is spiritual life and what he experience outside is simply a reflection of his inner real being which is awareness of consciousness. Therefore, the leader should live his life to full extent that will bring him to the situation of realizing perfection within him. Once he realizes his perfection, he will experience a true sense of joy which was missing in his work of leadership.

Hence, every leader is required to put his efforts in finding the inherent perfection within himself rather than spending his energy and time in outer world to be optimistic and positive. If we leave the idea of outer achievement, leave the ego which wants to be perfect, then it will bring us to a position of decisive great force for doing something good in the world.

People feel tired, fatigued in their work because they are unaware about the inner perfection within themselves. If the leader spends some more time in realization that beyond the commercial view of life there are the things from which he can bring most blissful and creative energy in his work performance. If he succeeded in his task of identifying the real source of perfection existed within, then automatically his material goals will get fulfilled and interactions with people will become blissful.

We all the time look at the perfections of other person, and when that other person's perfections does not meet our expectations, we feel unhappy. But, as per the Vedanta philosophy and spiritual science, we need to understand that at inner level we are a part of the same consciousness which every human being has. Hence, the spiritual aspect within all beings is always common in all of us. When a leader has a spiritual vision of looking at relationship with the people, all the problems about prestige, power and Egos goes away and genuine respect to all human being will come. His self-bliss shall bring him to the feeling that he is like a divine. When a leader understand this aspect of Vedadant philosophy and bring it into practice, he will be a stronger and a capable person of greater leadership value.

14. Self-Development

In a personality of any individual person, we basically see his personality in two parts – one is his outer personality i.e. external body appearance and the second is his inner part of personality. While understanding the outer part of personality, which is his physical body appearance, we also observe many other things with him, such as his ornaments, equipment, his dress, educational certificates and many other things in his possession which basically we call as his property items. Whereas, when we try to look into the inner personality of the same person, we experience certain qualities of his personality those are mainly his/her ability to think, capacity to understand and attitude to take action. But, in this regard we need to understand that these inner side qualities of a personality are not seen by our open eyes as those are invisible.

Leader's prime objective is to bring necessary change for developments of his followers personality. If an individual person understands his personality aspects in right perspectives, it will be easy for him to do his work activities in a better manner. Also, he will be able to know and understand his leader's personality in a better manner.

When we speak about the personality development of the employees working in an organization it means the development of their outer personality. We organize training programme taking into consideration the development of outer personality aspects of the individual body, dress code, knowledge, health, habits, skills, and many other aspects. But, all these aspects that we consider for development are basically physical things in nature and those are properties in possession of an individual. The second part of the human personality that we talk about is an inner personality of an individual which is '**SELF**' the 'Soul' in the body. We know that our external appearances which are outer personality aspects are in the form of material and physical in nature. This external personality can do movements here and there only if the real being that is 'Soul' remains alert and existing inside the body.

The outer personality that is body and other things with it can continue to do its movements as long as the **"Soul"** remains alert in the body. We need to believe that if the 'Soul' doesn't remain present in the body, our body remains as nothing but a log of a dead wood. In absence of the Soul inside the body, the outer personality aspects will be inactive. Hence, in reality we need to believe that the outer personality is just a reflection of our inner personality i.e. 'Soul'

'Vedanta' is the base of spiritual science texts i.e. Upanishad and out of it the 'Bhagavad Gita'. Lord Krishna, while talking to Arjun on basis of the Bhagavad Geeta on battle field i.e. 'Kuruksetra' he told that, the human body is a 'chariot' and the sense organs of the horses carrying the chariot is a "soul". The Bhagavad Gita also said that the body of a human being is like a dress/cloth and the 'Soul' inside body is the person who wears it. Hence, the Self-development means the development of the inner personality of an individual which is 'Self' or 'Soul' within. The 'Self' means nothing but our 'Atman' real being, pure consciousness exists in the Body itself. When we remember and become aware of the power of our consciousness in every activity and action, the infinite knowledge that is required for doing those activities will automatically come to help us in our action.

ୡୡୡ

15. Managing Self

'Vedanta' a spiritual science philosophy speaks about the real meaning of the word 'self' i.e. 'Soul' which we also call as our 'Atman'. The 'SELF' is also a part of our pure consciousness. It is an inner personality of a human being without which the outer or external body personality will be meaningless. If the 'soul' is absent in body, the outer personality remains inactive. In other words the outer personality is just a manifestation of our inner personality i.e. 'Soul'.

Leader's important duty is to develop the physical, mental and spiritual capacity of his followers, so that they will be inspired and motivated to do their works activities that are required for the well-being of human life. Developing spiritual capacity means awakening the 'SELF' which is already present in the human body. Leader needs to believe that the 'Self' itself is originally with infinite power to do any kind of good activity with a capacity to take any decision that necessary for a leader.

In real sense the 'SELF' itself will manage everything the way we want it if we awaken ourselves and become aware about the power of 'Self'. Therefore, the leader should always spend some time in developing his 'Self-Awareness'.

The "SELF" within human body has already an unending power to think, understand and to take decisions. **'SELF'** the secret inside the body has originally infinite power of decision making, high power of concentration and capability of immense acts of unselfishness. For taping these powers, we need to bring awareness within ourselves by practicing little bit Yoga and meditations. Development of human resources means helping a human being in bringing awareness about the power and capacity of the "SELF".

Teachings of the Swami Vivekananda the great Indian spiritual science philosopher told that "Education is nothing but manifestation of perfection which is already present in human soul". Therefore, managing

'Self' means bringing awareness of the perfection within the 'Self".

Keeping in view the above said ideology of spiritual science, every leader and his followers should think with a peaceful mind and required to plan for his own development in the following manner:

- Individual person, either he or she should do physical and mental exercises by practicing Yoga, and praṇayama on regular basis in order to keep himself/herself fit and strong.

- Human being by nature itself possesses the power of concentration, power of decision making and the power of unselfishness. Hence, every Individual person need to achieve and be aware of the said powers by maintaining mind calm, clean, pure and peaceful.

- Intellect power is present within every individual. We need to understand the said unending capacity of human mind by bringing awareness about the same.

- Once we set ourselves to develop the aforesaid three important powers already present in our personality, we become ready to do duties which are our responsibilities.

@@@

16. Spiritual Approach

'Vedanta' is a science of Indian spiritual world. It is a philosophy that speaks about the principles of human life styles, leadership, and success. Vedanta philosophy always with the corporate management theories and modern psychology. It is also in many ways a foundation of Japanese management system which is "Kaizen". We all know that during the third world war tragedy of Bomb attack on Hiroshima and Nagasaki in year nearby 1945, Japan was almost ruined. However, the same Japan nation awakened with full strength and courage and could bring back their economy very fast by doing hard work that made them to become advanced economically developed country of the world almost within a span of twenty years. Important secret behind this outstanding achievement is the implementation of the Japanese Management System i.e. Kaizen.

We have learned **'Vedanta'** philosophy and principles of spiritual science from the 'Upanishad' and 'Bhagwat Gita. It is a most essential teaching to learn by the Leaders who are functioning in any field of business and profession of the present world. 'Vedanta' philosophy teaches us that every human being is having a pure consciousness which is the divine power within. Hence, in order to realize our highest power and capability, we required to develop our awareness about the same. One thing we need to remember that every human being is a pure consciousness by nature itself. So, Vedanta is the highest spiritual truth that will bring us to the awareness of our consciousness and shall move us ahead fearlessly towards the complete self-actualization. 'Vedanta' is about making calm, peaceful mind and therefore it is very important for leaders to develop their potential realization with power of wisdom, and dynamism fearlessly in all situations.

Adi Shankaracharya, the great guru of Vedanta philosophy gave a clear cut idea of recognizing the divine within us. He says that all human beings are pure consciousness by nature itself. Hence, for realization of our highest capability the first thing that we must do is to bring awareness and know ourselves that we are divine a pure consciousness. But most of the time instead of knowing this truth of our real being i.e. divine power, we almost all human beings make mistake by becoming limited in scope. We restrict ourselves to our thoughts of mind and do act accordingly. We must understand that our pure consciousness is the master key for a dynamic leader that gives him infinite vision which is always beyond thoughts of mind. Vedanta tell us that we all human beings are having the power of pure consciousness and by becoming aware of the said infinite power we will succeed in living a higher quality of life. Therefore, the leader must know and understand essentially the power of divine available within him that will bring tremendous self-confidence which is necessary for him to become a successful leader.

We need to understand that the 'Vedanta' is not about a particular religion. it is about the realization of every human individual ultimate state of being which can be achieved by knowing or remembering the pure conscience power already within itself.

Every great leader should have vision of moving outside the cycle of his/her own thoughts. The

Leader need to believe and understand that his/her thoughts are on basis of the limited data that already collected in memory of mind. Therefore, the Leader should always have his vision beyond his thoughts. The leader who wish to be a successfully great leader, then he should always think out of the box of his own thoughts innovatively and dynamically.

17. Importance Of Honesty

Leader's role with reference to the term honesty is very important. While understanding major objectives of leader's functioning, we find that the leader has to motivate their followers and even people around them so that they will be inspired to do any kind of work activity that the leader wanted to do or get done. In order to get success in such a hectic exercise, leader is required to gain confidence of his followers which is possible only if he or she is honest. We need to keep in mind and remember that the Honesty is a value of each and every individual person by nature. Unfortunately, there are many exceptions to this statement. We find many dishonest people in business organizations, in industries and even in politics. But at the same time we also need to understand that the dishonest people are mainly because of the top positioned leaders, and it is a product of the dishonest culture and atmosphere in which the leaders and people are compelled to do their work activities.

We need to believe that a successful leader's personality is a bundle of various components of characters. Honesty is one of these characters, which can be seen through the personality of a leader as and when he starts functioning by doing any kind of work activity. In the present world of business organizations, we observe that the corruption is tremendously going on at various levels of the organizations which may be business, political, and even in social field of work. When we ask ourselves about the root cause to this problem the answer is lack of honesty.

Because of the corruptions being spread continuously everywhere, the human activities concerned with producing any kind of product or services for the wellbeing of human life are badly affected. This situation is arisen only because of the culture of corruption prevailing everywhere in the human societies. As there is a culture of dishonesty in many organizations in the world, the industries are unable to produce best quality goods and services.

As a consequence to this tragedy the progress of the economic development in every segment of business and industry is being crippled. Therefore every leader needs to endeavor to develop his followers by making them to understand and aware of the importance of honesty. For this most valuable task, leader must believe the principle that the charity should begin at home. It means the leader himself or herself should try to be honest first and then only he/she can teach honesty to others.

Education in school during our childhood taught us the lession of honesty to some extent while teaching the success stories of the great honest leaders. We use in works our knowledge, systems, principles, and experiences that we learned through our education. If it is so, then why many people do not use or bring in practice the lessions about the honesty that they learned through the educational system of institutions.

Hence, I request to all the leaders that, they should teach the importance of honesty to their followers. If the leaders are honestly putting their efforts in this direction, they will earn more capacity to function as the most successful leader in the present world. While understanding the importance of honesty we must believe that the quality of honesty can be nurtured, developed and even improved at any stage of human life.

ଚଚଚ

18. Knowing About Oneness

We see everywhere that the people on this earth are considering themselves separate and feel divided from most of the other people. In fact such kind of understanding is the basic problem in entire human being communities of the present world. Because of the understanding that there is no oneness in all the people, and each individual person is separate inner being consciousness, many conflicts amongst the people every now and then are happening and as a result of such situation the political and even religious institutions take advantages from that separateness to exploit the people's sense of insecurity.

The Vedanta philosophy, a text of the Indian spiritual science speaks about the concept of **oneness** in descriptive manner. According to the Vedanta, every human being belongs to the cosmos. The Atman i.e. soul is divine itself and it is a pure consciousness which is common in all human beings. The Great guru of Vedanta Adi Shankaracharya always emphasized about the oneness of human beings with others. The basic concept is each one of us is some portion of the universe. This implies that we all human beings are one with all the human beings within the cosmos. This is the basic truth of Vedanta and when we understand this truth, we will be able to change our entire perception about the world and we will stop looking at others as our enemies.

After knowing the truth of oneness and its importance, people will help each other and work together with cooperation which is the necessity of every successful leader in this world. This sense of cooperation shall create a great transformation in the minds of human beings. The concept of oneness will also bring closer to each other with the universe and spirituality. Every individual will feel a sense of joy enhancing quality of living that will help each other to work with happiness.

Leader's prime objective should be to encourage and inspire his people to get maximum cooperation in his task of doing the things which he wanted to do. In this context, all successful leaders must believe that the art of getting Cooperation from the people lies at the heart of human behavior. The only thing that we required to do is integration of consciousness rather than creating divisions amongst the people. This will be possible to a leader if he begin with an understanding that we are in oneness and a part of consciousness which is common to everyone. Because of our feeling of oneness, we suddenly become courageous with a great sense of confidence that moves towards vision of the leader for achievement of his goal.

19. Improve Will Power

The Leader who wishes to be a successful person in his functions must possess a strong will power. The prime objective of leader's functioning is to influence his followers and inspire them to do their assignments in best possible manner, enthusiastically, with willing cooperation to each other. This is necessary for helping their leader to make his vision true. Another important function of a leader is to take right kind of decisions at appropriate time. This is an extreme challenging task before a leader which is possible if he possesses a necessary and strong will power. At the same time, we must also agree that a leader can have adequate will power if he develops his knowledge, skill and an appropriate attitude through the work that he performs. Therefore, the real source of developing a strong will power is the work.

‘Will’ power and ‘confidence’ are natural phenomenon. However, to get it, one need to be aware of the same by developing and cultivating routine life style.

For this purpose, the leader must understand the important factors viz. (a) A fixed Goal. (b) Routine Life style and (c) Concentration.

The Leader can develop his will power with his sincere efforts by understanding above said factors in detail as explained here below, in right perspectives:

a) **Having a fixed Goal:** *Any person, either a Leader, Manager, political leader or any individual human being doing the work activities for achieving a particular objective,* or vision, need to possess a fixed determination in mind about the work activity to be done. Accordingly he/she must fix a definite goal and its objectives. Any person doing work activities without having a definite goal and objectives, such activities will be without any meaning and hence redundant. Most of the time we realize that, we produce thousands of unwanted thoughts in our mind in a second and such thoughts are irrelevant and therefore meaningless.

This happens because, most of the time human mind works like a hopping monkey.

If a Leader or any other person has a fixed and definite goal, he will focus only on that subject, and work only in that direction to achieve the results without thinking about anything else.

b) **Routine Life Style:** *While performing towards achievement of a definite goal and objectives, it is normal thing that he/she may come across with problems or will have to face disturbances and distractions in their work activities.* For avoiding such kind of disturbances, and to overcome the abnormal situations, one should develop a good, and ideal daily life style. We must be aware of the fact that, any kind of wrong life style of an individual brings many obstacles in working life.

Some of the things which are mainly responsible for wrong life style are viz.(i) habit of sleeping very late in night and getting up very late in the morning (ii) Irregular time of eating breakfast, lunch and even dinner, (iii) Spending morning time on viewing messages on 'Whats App' or other search media plat forms and attending unnecessary telephone calls. Instead, the Leader should spend his early morning hours doing some prayers, exercise or Yoga. (iv) Friendship with or accompany of wrong, irrelevant person of useless character.

The Leader, who pays attention to above four aspects of his life style, should seriously think about and improve upon for adopting a right kind of his own life style. The leader, who becomes successful in adopting a right kind of his routine life style, will be saving valuable time and will use the same time for doing some constructive work. He will also get mental peace which is necessary for developing will power and confidence.

c) **Concentration:** *We have very well learnt and understood the importance of concentration from Swami Vivekananda's teachings to entire human beings of the present world. He used to say that, hundred percent concentration of a man on any particular subject or idea,* gives him complete success.

Further, he said that, while doing any work activity or working on any idea, one should always think about that idea only and dream, and live with that particular idea paying his full attention, and concentration.

'**Vedanta**' *a science and philosophy of spirituality,* tell us that the awareness of mind status is the basic of self-realization. Therefore, the Leader, in addition to his concentration must also be aware of the state of mind condition that necessary to remain cool, pure, without any distractions while taking any kind of decision.

20. Work As A Play

While performing duty as a leader he should feel that he is doing the work activity for God. The God i.e. divine power already exists within every human being. Our "Soul" i.e. conscience is a part of God itself. Swami Vivekananda, a well-known leader of the Indian spiritual science and Vedanta philosophy always insisted every human being that the good work a man does as his duty, is a play of the divine. Swami Vivekananda never felt a sense of doer-ship of the work which he performed. He himself always looked at his work and his life as a very simple manifestation of God. With this kind of simple spiritual thinking, he created a strong positive psycho-spiritual vibration while he travelled many places in the world. The spiritual concept of Vedanta philosophy teaches us that the work and our existence is maximized by the awareness of our divine power that always expressed through the work activity we performed.

In other words, the work activity done by us is not of our own doing or own thinking, but, it is a simple expression of divine love manifested and expressed through our work activity that we do. If we do our work with the understanding and awareness that our work is an expression of divine love we will not feel the work activity that we perform is a burden or tiresome. This is what the principles of 'Vedanta' philosophy teaches us.

The work itself becomes worship and meditative in nature. Swami Vivekananda used to say that, even most of our very serious nature of duties should be performed in a way where the sense of **doer-ship** *disappears. The word* **'we'** *is required to be replaced with our feeling of working as a greater will power flowing through us. Therefore, while doing any kind of work activity which is basically our duty,* we required to keep on moving dynamically without any egoism motivation. Also, we should not have any kind of feeling or belief that we are limited by our own position, recognition or circumstances in the organization.

Most essentials of the idea of **"Karma Yoga"** *is removal of the sense of "doer ship" from our mind.* The "Karma Yoga" is the intellectual idea that the 'doer' word needs to be replaced with the existential idea that we are simply an expression of a greater reality divine power within us.

The Leader should unburden himself from his ego and get released from the idea of 'work' and 'non-work' 'action' and 'reaction'. Thereafter, he will have to move towards the situation where his inner being relates to the truth of the universe. The Leader is about the awareness of indestructible power of the universe that arising and overflowing within a person. He will move progressively towards the success in every sphere of activity in his life.

21. Awareness Of Thoughts

We learn from the 'Buddhist' philosophy that, if we do work with our inner awareness, happiness comes naturally. If we keep on investing ourselves only on outer pursuits, there will be only sorrow.

Leader's prime objective is to provide knowledge and guide his followers appropriately to do their work activities in a best possible manner. Followers are required to perform well so as to make their leader's vision true and successful. For this purpose, the leader should motivate and inspire people to do work efficiently and effectively with the cooperation of all in the team. Every person while functioning as a Leader comes across the crises situations and if he is able to deal with such crises situation with full awareness and understanding of spiritual power that is consciousness, he will be definitely able to achieve success by overcoming to such crises situation. But, if he deals with the same situation keeping himself too close with his point of view with the outer objectives, he may commit many mistakes.

Many Leaders gets entangled in their anxious thoughts avoiding the awareness of their essential being. They are unable to understand that, those anxious thoughts are not their real thoughts. Because a man is not a biophysical mind and body. It is a realization about the leader's essential being and awareness which is established in his mind. Therefore, the huge energy empowers leaders to perceive things as they truly are, and not the way their thoughts have suggested them. Awareness about the essential being i.e. **'Atman'** *is something which is at the heart of the leader's spiritual and mystical search. The awareness implies enjoying moments of life through an absorption in what happening and not an absorption in the mind's thoughts, perceptions and imagining. The leader, whose duty is to inspire his followers to do work with each other's cooperation which required his open awareness rather than closed thoughts.* Essentially, greatest ability of a leader is the ability to establish deep contacts with his team through which others come in relationships with teamwork.

It does not matter whether the contacts are at level of a business network, at the level of political organization or any level of a social organization. It is all about making heart to heart contacts with people.

Most important thing for the leaders to understand here is, their lots of energies are being wasted in the confusion of meaningless and irrelevant thoughts. In fact, the efficient and effective leaders are those who do not fight with their own thoughts. The most successful leaders reconcile their own thoughts and always remain peaceful within them. If the Leader himself is calm, and quite with peaceful mind, only then he will be able to guide his followers, effectively and successfully. Ultimately, very important thing is as to how leadership quality and skill of a leader impress upon his followers at the time of leading them to perform the work. Therefore, the Leader is required to learn how to leave aside the heavy burden of unnecessary, irrelevant thoughts and just go beyond to those thoughts by investing time in openness and awareness.

22. Never Be Invincible

'Leader' becomes a successful person by achieving excellent results after functioning as a good leader of his followers. Obviously, it is natural for him to think as a most powerful person. Because he is the winner and we call him as a **Vijeta.** *But, before he or she gets such kind of feeling in mind, he is required to think that his victory or the success that he achieved is a temporary phenomenon.* In fact, such kind of feeling and understanding that he is the winner and therefore a powerful person, it is his wrong perception. Because, he being a conqueror a **'Vijeta'** *must realize that such kind of his feeling about victory takes away his ability to be discerning.*

'EGO' *always ends up making wrong choices. Making wrong choices is a most terrible thing that any egoistic leader may do. Therefore, a successful leader should not get crowded with the clouds of* *his thoughts that continually remind him about his ultimate conquerorship.*

This situation ultimately takes him to 'Ego' state of mind without allowing him to go to the greater sky of infinity.

Instead, a leader should go into the clarity of seeing things beyond his clouds of self-importance and should raise him higher and higher that will take him to do something good.

The position of power and wealth – all these come and go. The only thing which is eternal, permanent and timeless is consciousness. The Bhagwat Gita, which is most complete text of spiritual science given to us by the 'Vedanta' philosophy and 'Upanishad' which are being practiced all over the world including our country Bharat, is all about the consciousness. It is for Leader to understand that, he essentially required to be free from the Ego. He, being a 'Winner' of the battle should not have feeling that he is above everybody being a winner of the battle. The truth is always with a person who is without any ego, and it does not consider himself to be a supreme just because of the merits and his skills alone.

Sometime, people also think that they are better only because they possess a better set of skill and knowledge. But in real sense, most of the time it is also seen in life that the calmness and coolness of a person also leads him to achieve all-round victory.

The Leaders who remain away from the idea of identifying themselves on basis of their position, the victory that they achieved, and by leading people with their personal power, will hardly lose anything. The leaders having understood the importance of the human consciousness which is 'SELF' explained under 'Vedanta philosophy' will always look forward to do the things by a new eye, and so doing better with feeling that they are almost undefeatable. In this very sense of capability, they are free from 'Ego' mind and do work with the real feeling of heart. By getting such kind of awareness in their mind, they become surer about themselves for functioning as a leader for a maximum degree of satisfaction.

Hence, a Leader, whoever and wherever he/ she may be or he may be belongs to any kind of organization must understand that he should not carry with himself the foolish pride, and must always be humble, gracious, dignified and strong enough for leading his followers with a successful leadership.

ꝍꝍꝍ

23. A Good Listener

Basically, the art of deep listening means focusing attention to the higher consciousness existing within us. Having deep listening to the subject of any kind, one gets an inner relation and real understanding of reality. True intelligence means being free from any kind of conditioning, and responding to the things as we experience them. The real transformation comes through the inner absorption and insight into how things really work. The responsibility of a good leader is to remain alert in any situation. In fact, primary duty of a leader is to create order where there is chaos.

The science of spirituality i.e. Vedanta philosophy said that a person needs to think and find the original self [i.e. Atman]. The Atman is hidden underneath conditioning with several layers. Listening attentively allow us to feel those layers and to peel them out.

Ultimately we come to the core, a power of our Atman which we also said as 'Atmagyan.'

Vedanta philosophy also says that while listening in a deep and gross manner, the subtle art of deeper listening comes to an inner silence and telling us to act from that inner silence.

Further to this, the Vedanta philosophy says that we live with many circles inside of life. The outer most circle is the material objects of outer world. Within that circle there is another circle which is the circle of our own physical being. Within that also there is another circle of our thoughts or our ideas. Thereafter, the circle of our own feelings and then the circle of the pure 'witness' within us. This pure witness is the purest of things within. So, it is our duty at the inner most core to listen to these different circles and layers of our existence. If we listen close enough to the people and events in the material world, we come closer to our thought process and we begin to understand our own feeling better. Ultimately, we are able to access our core inner most intelligence of being a pure witness i.e. power of SELF.

The act of listening with deep attention is very important for effective functioning of a leader. Spirituality is a growth process, and in order to grow, we required to put our entire heart and mind for getting great intensity. In fact, intensity is one of the hallmarks of good leadership. Without intensity one remains unsure. Intensity means wholeness and totality of our being which is born from the act and art of listening totality. It is born from bringing higher consciousness to our listening.

@@@

24. Significance Of Spirituality

Importance of the principles of spirituality explained in Upanishad. 'Vedanta' philosophy an Indian spiritual science is also an essential concept of spirituality to understand the Leadership and the effectiveness of a leader. Because, these principles tell us about the mental strength of a leader who takes many decisions while functioning as a leader.

When we try to understand the significance of spirituality under Vedanta philosophy and its Upanishad, we get clear idea of the divine i.e. God exist within every human being. For a Leader to become successful in his functioning, it is very important for him/her to know and understand the divine power and self-awareness which is already present within him. This divine power gives enough strength, and confidence to a leader for fighting with any difficult situation that he comes across. It helps him to overcome any problem situation that arises in his functioning as a leader. After knowing the importance of spirituality under the Vedanta philosophy, the leader become aware of the pure consciousness and then take all challenges fearlessly with a full strength and courage. A leader with self-awareness of pure consciousness is dynamic, and confident that lead him to get success.

The very important message to learn from the spiritual science under Vedanta is the **"God"** *the 'Atman' which is pure consciousness,* and we all human beings are an integral part of it. So, we must realize and understand that, behind the material world around us, there is great power of wealth which is a consciousness that is helping us to function as a leader to meet all our objectives.

It is very important that every leader must identify him as an essential being of pure consciousness. Because, the leader has a special role of inspiring his followers and to guide them properly for doing the work activities effectively and in a best possible manner. The great scientists of the world have also said that, the Upanishad under 'Vedas' are a product of a mysterious high consciousness energy that is a life.

Therefore, every leader is required to know the consciousness and infinite self-confidence existing within him which will give success in achieving the higher quality of life. 'Gautama Buddha' also said that the human capacity of consciousness, infinite energy creates a broad vision of leadership. For knowing the higher spiritual nature of human being, one must go beyond the ordinary complexes and habits of the mind.

@@@

25. Build High Performance

Prime objective of a leader is to inspire, influence the employees to produce the goods and services that necessary for wellbeing of human life and to achieve the targets of the organization. It is also true to say that, for availing this success, the leader needs to motivate and encourage his people so as to get necessary efficiency from the employees to work effectively, willingly, by extending cooperation to the entire team at work place.

For the purpose of creating a high performing team of his employees the leader is required to take following steps:

1. Organizing need base intensive training programme for the employees at shop floor of the organization. This activity is very essential to upgrade every employee skill, knowledge,

experience that will bring right kind of attitude towards the work activity that the employee do on regular basis. Training activities are also helping in improving employee work efficiency and enable them to do the work in a best possible manner.

2. After returning back in the organization from the training programme every employee's expectation is that, he should be given a fair, proper treatment with love, sympathy, and compation.

   Hence, the leader should take needful step in this regard very promptly.

3. Employees working for any organization always want to know about their career path in the organization. This they require to understand very authentically in addition to the salary package that they earn. The employee while doing every work activity in the organization, always seems to be ambitious about his next position and grade. After working for more and more days in the same organization, he will be looking at the position presently working and will expect about his next promotion

and placement. Also, he will be desirous to know about his future growth possibility and prosperity in the organization for which he is working.

4. Transparency, simplicity and clarity in communication system of management is very important for managerial functioning of an organization. Because, these aspects play very essential role in determining the competency of a leader and employees.

   The Leader when he makes his efforts to communicate every item of his functioning to his followers, it is important to see that the employees have fully understood, listened and agreed to the message conveyed to them by their leader.

   In regard to the transparency, simplicity and clarity in communication system, it is important to know that the message which was communicated to the employees was listened, understood by them properly, and the employees had a feeling that there was no any ambiguity or favoritism about the said message. Leader should always remain alert, and careful about the situation arising out of and due to the miscommunication. Leader should also deal with the complaints received from the employees in regard to favoritism. For achieving objectives of transparences in managerial functioning, it is necessary for a leader to take some initiative action so as to bring some improvement in the communication systems of the organization.

5. The organization should always give first preference to its internal employees while doing the recruitment against the existing vacancy position of a higher grade employee.

   Leader should always encourage and give preference to the deserving candidates available within the organization and waiting for promotion to the higher position.

6. Participation in management functions is a most crucial aspect of an employee motivation. Therefore, the Leader should be always keen to involve his employees in the decision-making process of the organization.

@@@

26. Culture Of Team Spirit

Inspiring followers and people around for doing work activities efficiently, effectively, enthusiastically and willingly is an important duty of a leader. For this purpose, it is also essentially important that the leader or a manager who manage such kind of activities, possess sufficient knowledge about the process of team building of the employees at work. The employees/workmen doing their works activities for the organization with a team spirit brings positive synergy at work place. It is an accepted fact that the work activity done by an employee in a team is always greater than the work performed by him individually without a team.

Teams Vs. Group*:*

- *Two or more individuals interacting with each other to do work together for achieving a common goal is a group. Group members interact with each other, sharing information and helping each other in a group in order to realize the goals. However, while doing such kind of exercise towards achievement of a success the employees does not engage themselves in their work activities that would lead to* **a joint well-coordinated effort**.

Hence, their performance is just equal to the sum total of individual employee contribution.

Teamwork *has a synergistic effect to achieve more than the individuals working alone in a group. Teamwork does not just happen; it requires continuous efforts to build. The Leader should inform team members that the team interest is above personal aspirations and the results of team work shall give a feeling of personal satisfaction to each and every team member. Team members exchanges their feelings, opinions, ideas openly and discuss freely to learn from each other. The pride and a sense of belongingness provide motivation to the team members.*

BUILDING A TRUST:

In order to be a successful team, it is essentially required to create a trustworthy atmosphere in the organization. The leader must put his efforts in bringing trust in him and in the minds of his team members about the people. The Leader is also required to trust in the people's integrity, ability, loyalty and character with him as a leader of the team. The Leader working on the task of building a trust in his followers needs to keep in mind the following few things:

- The manager/leader should demonstrate that he is working for the interest of others and then for himself.
- The manager/leader shall whole heartedly support his team members as and when there is attack on them from any out sider person.
- The manager/leader shall explain and keep informed to every member of the Team about the decisions that he has taken in the interest of team works.

- The manager/leader appreciates the team members who perform well and avoid thoughtless comments.
- The manager/leader should guide his team members by making them to understand the subject and providing adequate knowledge with necessary skills through technical competence, interpersonal skills and team building process. The Leader should also explain to the team members about the importance of team spirit in the functions of management.

ஐஐஐ

27. Stress Management

Leader's main objective is to motivate, influence, and inspire his followers to do their work activities enthusiastically. While doing this exercise, it is most important for a leader to understand about the stressful conditions of his employees while performing the works activities in a different kind of environmental situation. If an individual is caught with a stressful situation, he will be unable to maintain his health in a good condition and consequently it will be difficult for him to give justice to his work activities in an effective manner.

Basically, the stress is a condition of an individual person's mind which has mainly happened because of the ignorance of the importance of work that he does. The stress also arises because of various kind of working conditions including environment in which the individual employee does his work.

If the stress of a person is a condition of mind because of his unawareness of the importance of his work and hazardous conditions of work, then the leader need to explain to his employees/followers exactly as to what are the work activities about and what are the duties Involved therein and why a person required to do those work activities as a matter of his duty and responsibility.

While talking to the employees about their work activities and responsibility it is very essential for the leader to inform his followers that the work is worship and they need to do the same as if they do prayer or puja of their 'God' at home,

> The spiritual principles under Vedanta philosophy teaches us the importance of work i.e. **"KARMA YOG"** *and our duty towards the said karma. The philosophy said that every individual human being of this world has to do the work which may be good or bad. If an individual person does a good work, then it is considered as his duty and therefore it is his or her devotion to the religion i.e. "***Dharma***". If a person does bad work, then it is against the principles of*

*his/her religion and therefore it is considered as "***Adharma***" However, every individual person who does any kind of good work must be aware of himself that the work that he performs being his duty needs to be performed with unselfish motive. It means he or she who did that particular good work should not expect anything return or any benefit from that work. Because he/she has offered the said good work activity to the 'God' itself through his worship.*

Therefore, the duty performed by the employee of an organization without any expectation of benefits and with unselfish motive is a **'Karma Yoga'** *which goes to the god directly as worship.*

The principle of "Karma Yoga" given in Vedanta philosophy and the importance of work done as worship needs to be appreciated by the Leader with a great interest and he should be able to convey the same to the employees and his followers. The principle of 'Karma Yoga' that we understood is also a message of 'Bhagwat Gita' an Indian spiritual science. If the employees are told appropriately and made to understand the importance of

'Karma Yoga' in right perceptive the employees themselves will be able to find the solution to the problem of their stress. Because, the stressful condition of an individual is a condition of his mind which is mainly due to the misunderstanding of the importance of his work activities. The Leader in his efforts of conveying the concept of "Karma Yoga" to his employees, he also required to explain and make them understand the few important things given here below in order to help them to overcome their stressful situation.

- Every individual person is basically made of three parts –(1) physical body, (1) mind, and (3) intelligence i.e. Buddhi. The '**Atman**' *which is a pure consciousness is over and above these three aspects. The stress which we talk about is the condition of mind caused by various kinds of irrelevant, unwanted thoughts in the mind.*

- The stress of mind and physical body is mainly because of irrelevant thoughts clouded and gathered unnecessarily in mind.

- The stressful condition of mind may be because of the occupational hazards creating unpleasant atmosphere. Individual employee while working in the said situation becomes irritable, leading to unstable behavior, heavy smoking, psychosomatic pains, depression, and fatigue and drug abuse.

- Therefore, the Leader needs to understand such things very seriously and after becoming aware of such situation, he must take necessary steps through HR-Manager for reducing the pressure of stressful condition that has arisen basically due to the occupational hazards conditions.

- The stressful condition can be avoided if any good work i.e. Karma is done as a 'worship' offering to the God with an unselfish motive.

֍֍֍

28. Quality Of Work Life

Most important responsibility of a successful leader is giving assurance to his followers about the quality of their work life. This kind of assurance is essentially necessary from a leader to his followers because he has to acquire willing response and cooperation from them to perform the work activities enthusiastically, efficiently, and effectively.

The quality of work life means the quality of working relationship between the employees and the total working environment of the place where the employees do their work. Every employee shall be ambitious to-do his work willingly and effectively if he get assurance of human dignity, and growth of his career. Therefore, the Leader of every organization is required to design the work activities of each employee keeping in mind the following few things so that the employee doing his work will be able to get the quality in his work life:

a) Adequate salary/remuneration package, incentives and benefits.

b) Providing a proper opportunity to the employees in order to enable them to maintain their physical and mental health.

c) Evolving a system for identifying employee stress and problems arising due to the hazardous conditions at work place. Also providing necessary remedies for overcoming to the stress situation.

d) Providing career growth opportunities to the employees at work so that they can develop themselves in their professional and personal life. The employees should also be given an opportunity to accept higher positions in the organization so that they can gain confidence in accepting responsibilities.

e) Employees need to be provided with appropriate training facilities especially working in technical field, good communication skills, and good behavioral science. The employees should also be given adequate opportunities to represent themselves for speaking about himself and such talk should be heard carefully. Management should give necessary time to the Employee for discussing his goals

®®®

29. Potential Appraisal

While introducing potential appraisal system for employees in the organization, the Leader needs to take the following important steps:

a) Preparing Job-Description of each employee, defining role of each individual employee in the organization.

b) Functions and expectations from the employee in regard to the quality of the works done should be spell-out before the job is performed by the employee. The management should also have the appropriate mechanism for judging the qualities of employees in terms of their technical knowledge, managerial competencies, and abilities to perform the job,

c) Employee's record in regard to his initiative, creativity and risk-taking capacity in employment career needs to be maintained.

d) Management should have policy decisions about the weightage of merit in place of seniority while giving promotions to the employees.

The organization should have the procedure of conducting interview in order to provide an opportunity to the employees to speak about their performance. Also, there should be a system for knowing the results of assessment of employee performance appraisals done by the Manager under the potential appraisal system of the organization.

The manager should also inform to his employee's interviews results after the potential appraisal job is done. Thereafter, employees should also be provided with necessary help in understanding about the quality of work that was expected by management from its employees.

&&&

30. IMPLEMENT 'KAIZEN'

Global market conditions of the present business scenario prevailing in the present world have compelled every industrial organization to produce world class quality goods and services in order to enable them to survive successfully in its business. This particular message in regard to the quality of goods and services is for each and every industrial unit of business organization. Also, it is more necessary for each and every individual who struggle for their well-being and better quality of life.

In this context, every Leader of the organization must learn and understand the principles of the **"Kaizen"** i.e. Japanese Management system and should endeavor to implement the same philosophy for his organization, followers, and himself.

Producing quality goods and services is an order of the day of present business world competitions. Hence, every progressive business organization must accept this particular aspect of quality as a challenge. The Leader of every industrial organization should also teach the concept of "Kaizen" to his employees/followers and implement the same in the organization for better quality product and services.

Japan is a nation which was almost ruined during the Second World War after attacks on Hiroshima and Nagasaki in 1945. Thereafter, within a period of 15 to 20 years Japan became an advanced country of the world in regard to its progress in the field of technology and in development of economy.

"KAIZEN" is a Japanese management system. The word 'Kai' stands for change and the word 'Zen' stands for better. The complete meaning of the word KAIZEN in English language is a 'change for better'. It also stands for a continuous improvement. "Kaizen" improves flexibility of the Business as a whole by taking challenges of global competition. 'Kaizen' establishes able leadership in business and industrial organizations. 'Kaizen' allows every individual person in the organization to contribute for overall improvement of the work efficiency and effectiveness. 'Kaizen' also provides an opportunity to each and every individual to do improvements in his/her personal, social and working life activities. ''Kaizen' provides a platform and also an audience to each individual person wherein he/she can make his contribution by giving presentation on any subject of improvement related to the human activities of their choice.

"KAIZEN" is a philosophy of approach that helps a person to improve the quality of human life by using all resources efficiently and effectively. 'Kaizen' gives importance to very small improvements rather than big one that are concerned with the day to day quality of human life.

"KAIZEN" is a system that gives importance to even 'Zero' improvement.

The basic idea of the Kaizen philosophy is to involve as many people as possible in the process of improvement activities so that they all can get converted into stars of better performance in future.

"KAIZEN" is for quality consciousness. It believes in small and smaller improvements involving therein more and more people. 'KAIZEN' helps in molding the behavior of the people at work in a positive direction and builds right kind of attitude for doing the activities for producing quality goods and service.

Though the "KAIZEN" is the Japanese management system, the industrial organizations in India must implement the same if they intend to improve the quality of their goods and services at bare minimum cost.

Hence, each and every individual who is in charge of the Leadership in any kind of industrial, business and political activities must learn the 'Kaizen' of the Japanese Management System and should also implement the same for the employees of the organization to whom he/she leads.

31. Develop Human Relations

Activities of each and every industrial and even business organization are basically depending upon the functions of the factors of production that are mainly – a) Manpower b) Material c) Money d) Marketing and e) Management. Among these five factors, the first one i.e. Manpower is the most important factor out of all other four factors of production. The term manpower means the total number of employees working in the organization. It is related to and concerned with the human emotional aspects. Therefore, the techniques, remedies' and even methods of motivations adopted for improving the effectiveness and efficiencies of all other four factors are not identical or similar to those used to improve the effectiveness and efficiency of the employees.

Managing employees at work place is primarily concerned with the understanding of human emotions in relation to their needs, aspirations and expectations about which human relations are dependent.

In order to have ideal human relations with the employees at work place, management of the organization is required to implement various kinds of welfare policies and incentives schemes which are for motivation of employees at all level of the organization. While implementing employee welfare schemes, management need to give more preference in settlement of the issues on subjects like employee conflict resolution, employee grievances handling, and the procedure of employee complaints resolution.

Human Relations: Good investment in maintaining and improving human relations is a one of the best kinds of investment. Because of the diversity of interests, views, and values of different groups of individuals, many difficulties are arising in building up human relationships.

A group of employees with motivation, enthusiastic, and willingness to do the work is a basic necessity of every organization to meet the challenges of work performances.

Therefore, the leader needs to take initiatives at all level to motivate and take his employees in confidence by providing them the human welfare facilities.

For achieving this particular objective, the Leader should also involve his followers/employees in various activities of the organization by sharing the information to them wherever possible and necessary.

Employee Morale: Motivation leads to bring confidence among the employees to perform well. Finally, this helps in building a high employee morale condition in the organization. The relationship between motivation and morale is very close to each other. Hence, employees of high morale condition can do wonders in the human relations situation of the organization. The volume of achievements of people depends upon the level of moral in a group of the people at work.

The **Leader** being a representative of the management, should endevour to motivate his people by providing to them the basic things of necessities that required for the wellbeing of human life and after resolving employee grievances promptly so as to increase the level of overall morale conditions of the employees to perform well.

®®®

32. Importance Of Character

Leader is a person who makes his vision true with the cooperation and help of his followers. Leader's vision includes his objectives of getting work done from his people who are with him to do the work activities willingly, enthusticaly and with each other's cooperation. But, every individual person is unable to do his work willingly on his own because of inadequate knowledge, right kind of aptitude and experience that he requires to do his work activities efficiently and effectively for producing best quality of goods and services.

Therefore, for every organization either it is industrial, social or even political field organization engaged to do any kind of good work activities needs a leader having capacity, competency that enable him to bring within him a good moral character. The good character of a leader always helps him to lead his employees by inspiring them to do their work effectively with necessary knowledge, behavioral skills and experiences.

Leadership is an abstract quality of an individual person to inspire his people around to do whatever they are directed to do with a zeal and confidence.

It is an influence of a particular individual's personal power, and behavior that creates progressively advancing community towards common purpose. Leadership is not a power that has been acquired by a person because of his position as like a manager or a director in the organization.

Leadership is a force of an organization that designs, executes, coordinate and control all functions. It is a dynamic and a major attribute that gives life to an organization for its success. The qualities that determines good character of a Leader are as follows:

CHARACTERISTICS OF A LEADER:

- It is a personal quality of an individual that influences behavior of his followers.

- Leader is a person who also influences his own behavior, and behaviour of other people around him to join up and move out with him. This can be understood appropriately by knowing the quality of a successful leader of any organization including the leader of political organization.

- Good health conditions of a leader are determined by the status of his physical, mental and spiritual strength.

- Foundation of a good moral character of a leader is his positive thinking power that is required for overcoming all difficulties of human life. A person's vision towards achieving goals of good communication skill, high level capacity of self- motivation is also a part of good moral character.

- A Leader must develop a behavior which is exhibited through his style of work that willingly accepted by his followers.

- A Leader can acquire a good qualities of his personality that builds his character by doing his work activities consistently with sincerity, honesty and in a dignified manner. Leadership is a reciprocal relationship between a Leader and his followers.

- Leadership is a continuous process of influencing behavior of leader's followers.

- Leadership is an action taken in relation to a particular situation arisen at a given point of time under a specific set of circumstances.

- Leader is a guide for his followers doing their work activities towards achievement of a predetermined common goal.

- Leadership is something a person does as a leader and not something he possess as a person. Leadership qualities and characteristics is seen through actions of a leader.

@@@

33. Functions Of A Leader

Leader is a key person of an organization. It is true that the people engaged by the organization as its employees are having adequate knowledge, skill and experiences. But, if we want to inspire the employees to do their work willingly, efficiently, and effectively for producing good results, then they will need proper guidance, directions and control from their leader who is with skill of managing behavior of people at work.

Therefore, every organization need a person who possesses the qualities that mentioned here below to function as an effective leader having the responsibility of leading employees at work place.:

QUALITIES OF A GOOD LEADER:

- Status of good health with a sound mental, and physical fitness. A person, who is having a strong-physical structure of his body, can also enjoy a sound mind condition that necessary to do many wonders while functioning as a leader.

- Leader should possess quality of honesty, sincerity, integrity, dignity and good moral character.

- If a person lacking these important qualities, he will be like a building which is constructed without using sand, steel, stone, and cement which may collapse at any moment of time.

- Leader’s most important function is to inspire, influence and motivate his followers to do their job willingly and enthusticaly with cooperation to each other. Hence, the leader needs to be intelligent enough and should himself remain always enthusiastic with a self-disciplined character.

- Leader need to gain confidence of people to whom he leads. Therefore, he needs to have friendliness relationship with his followers maintaining faith, and cooperation with each other.

- Managing people for getting work done to produce good results is an important function of a manager being a leader. Therefore, a leader should also possess the knowledge of managerial skills.

- The Leader having good character always commands confidence, and respect from his followers to do the various kinds of works activities towards the achievement of his goals and fulfillment of his vision.

IMPORTANCE OF A GOOD LEADER:

- Leader is a person whose responsibility is to pull out the organization from darkness to light.

- Leader is a person in an organization who can manage entire gamut of work activities by its effective functioning as a leader to achieve success.

- Leader is an essential person of the organization who motivates employees at work place. Therefore, he need always to upgrade and enhance his capacity to do well.

- Leadership of an organization directs the efforts of people at work in right direction towards the achievement of the organizations goals

- Leadership builds high morale conditions that bring voluntary cooperation of the employees at work.

- Leadership mobilizes workforce to get higher performance in organization.

- Leadership develops talents of the employees by promoting self-confidence in them.

34. Mind Management

Human being appearance is basically in three parts – (1) Physical structure i.e. Body. (2) Mind and (3) Intelligence which is named as Buddhi. The fourth one is 'Atman' that is SELF and it is pure consciousness. It is an inner power that is an awareness always shining through body, mind and Buddhi. The first component that is Body always functioning for manifestation of the functions of mind and Buddhi. The consciousness which is divine power, always seen through the functioning of mind and Buddhi. If the functioning of mind stopped due to the distractions of any kind that may come across because of the clouds of overburdening flow of irrelevant, unnecessary thoughts gathered in mind, then the functioning of physical body also stops.

The 'Atman' i.e. **"SELF"** being, a divine power of consciousness always manifested through the functions of mind and intelligence. Hence, consciousness is the foundation of mind. If the mind condition is pure then the divine inner power shall be manifested through the functions of mind.

Therefore, we should always try to keep our mind free from any kind of distractions which are crowded because of the irrelevant, unwanted and redundant thoughts.

In order to have the functioning of pure mind conditions, every Leader should practice few **steps** given here below, so as to have organized mind conditions with minimum distractions:

1. Leader should watch his rate of breathing frequently. For this purpose, he needs to practice 'PRANAYAMA' of Patanjali Yogsutra. If he finds his breathing rate High, then it is because of the distractions in mind functions.

2. Bringing down the high rate of breathing, means removing all kinds of irrelevant, unwanted thoughts accumulated in mind.

3. In order to have calm, quiet and pure peaceful mind condition, then the leader should watch

his entire thought process and he Should delete the irrelevant thoughts unnecessarily gathered, clouded in his mind?

Thereafter, he needs to keep only few useful relevant and essential thoughts by removing all other unwanted thoughts.

4. After seeing and then removing all irrelevant, unwanted thoughts from the mind, the leader required to take next step of bringing some new thoughts in mind as a replacement to earlier thoughts which were removed. The new thoughts brought in mind must be most relevant, necessary and very selective for his purpose of life.

Leader will be able to get his organized mind conditions after implementation of the above said four steps by himself. If he hesitates to organize his mind in the manner mentioned in the above said four steps, then his mind conditions will remain all the time unorganized and as a result of the said situation he will not be able to enjoy the purity and cheerful condition of his mind condition that is essentially required for the awareness of his real being pure consciousness existing inside to take right kind of decisions in his capacity as a leader.

@@@

35. A Successful Leader

Every leader having desire to become a successful person in his task of leadership must be aware of the following few things in his functioning as a leader.

1. Leader need to spend some time in collecting the details about the subject and his position which he uses to lead people for inspiring them to do the work activities towards the accomplishment of his targets.

2. Leader as and when situation demands, must cultivate his habit of showing willingness to do the work activities along with his followers.

3. Leader need to be aware about and agree to the principle that, he earns his salary for the work that he does and not for the work he knows.

4. Leader must develop his ability of getting the work done from his followers. An able personality of a leader greatly influences his people with his magnetism and working knowledge to do their work activities in a better way of manner.

5. Leader's loyalty towards his associate is most important aspect in achieving success. Leader need to be loyal with the people those above him and to those who are below him.

6. Leader is known by his nature of conduct, character and understanding that demonstrate fairness of his job. The efficient leader always enlightens his people by leading with encouragement and motivation.

7. Leader is not necessarily required to possess a big "Title" of his position for gaining more respect from his followers. A successful leader always keeps his door open for listening to his followers.

8. Leader need to have the well-defined purpose of his life and a definite fixed goal to achieve.

9. Leader should be a self-disciplined person. He must restrain all negative qualities by controlling himself.

@@@

36. LEADERSHIP

A leader is a person who has a vision. He makes his vision come true with the cooperation of his followers. For getting necessary cooperation from his followers, he needs to be with certain qualities, possess abilities, and responsibilities which are as given here below.

- Leader must possess adequate knowledge, skill, and a particular behavior pattern that necessary for influencing, encouraging and inspiring his followers to do work activities.

- Leader is with an intense power within himself. He needs to be aware of and use the same for overcoming to any critical situation.

- Leader should adopt a management style of work with a proper behavior so that followers will do work activities in a best possible manner.

- Leader need to possess a strong will power which is developed by himself after cultivating his routine life style.
- Leader should always believe that the work he does is as a matter of his duty and responsibility. He must also believe that the work is a worship to the God.
- Leader has to deal with any kind of situation with full awareness of his consciousness.
- Leader, when he gets success should not enjoy as a conqueror. Because such kind of feeling takes away his ability to be discerning.
- Leader's habit of listening close to the people and events in the material world will help him to bring out his core inner most intelligence i.e. power of 'SELF'
- Leader should believe and be aware of the fact that the power of divine gives strength to deal with any problematic situation.

- Lord Gautama Buddha said that the human consciousness is with infinite energy which gives a broad vision of leadership.

- Leader need to build a high performing team by providing training, fair treatment and career growth opportunities to his employees.

- Leader should inform to his people that the Vedanta philosophy taught us that the work activity is a worship to the God.

- Leader to provide his followers the quality of working relationship between employees and the environment including relations with management.

- Leader should do the potential appraisal of his employees after preparing job-description and quality standards of work in a scientific manner.

- Leader need to implement "KAIZEN" Japanese Management System which helps every individual to improve the quality of work and human life as well.

- Leader need to design motivation policy only after understanding his employee emotions in relation to their needs as a human being.
- Leadership with a good moral character is a force that designs, executes and control functions of an organization.
- Leader should maintain friendly relationship with his followers so as to earn their confidence.
- Leader need to keep his mind free from distractions of irrelevant, redundant thoughts frequently gathered in mind.
- Leader should listen to the voice that coming from his real being pure consciousness within.
- Leader must give priority to self-awareness. It is 'SELF' i.e. Atmagyan gives energy to create excellence.
- Leader to influence followers on basis of personal power which he gets from his personality traits.
- Leader functioning after realization of SELF within, gives confidence to his followers.

- Leader with his consciousness is with highest capacity of courage, energy and self-confidence. He is a 'GURU' for himself.
- Leader has to do something extraordinary which will encourage and inspire his people around.
- Leader must teach discipline to his followers believing that the discipline is backbone of every organization.
- Leader always need to keep mind cool. If he has aggressive mind he may lose his consciousness that may lead to any kind of disaster.
- Leader must be honest. He should develop and improve the quality of honesty of people with him.
- Leader should spend time in finding perfection within him instead of wasting energy and time in outer world.
- Leader must believe that the Self-Development means developing awareness of consciousness within.

- Leader need to believe that the 'Self' itself is infinite power to do any kind of work. For taping these powers we simply need to be awaken ourselves with awareness.
- Leader should have a vision to move outside the cycle of his own thoughts by thinking innovatively and dynamically.
- Leader to learn Vedanta philosophy which is the highest spiritual truth that brings awareness of consciousness and self-actualization.

@@@

37. Leader Is Mentor

The 'Leader' in the role of a Mentor can assess the strength and weakness of his followers and can point out to them the actual areas where they need to do the improvement. Hence, the Leader needs to play a Mentor's role for providing expert knowledge to his followers which he possess from his personal experiences. A Leader, in his capacity as a good Mentor may do well and can achieve success in his role of a Mentor if he develop the qualities such as:

- Mentor need to possess reliable expert knowledge which he gained on basis of his experiences, maturity and wisdom.
- Leader in his capacity as a Mentor should play as a role model leading by examples.

- Leader, while in his role as a Mentor, must be available to his followers whenever they need him.

- Leader in Mentor role need to be a trusted advisor, friend, and a teacher for his followers

- Mentor should keep away his followers from committing mistakes.

- Mentor is as if a 'GURU' as per the spiritual science. A genuine guru should be theoretically erudite and practically realized.

Why we required a Leader in the role of a Mentor?

Following are some widely acknowledged reasons:

1. **Mentor** provides with distilled knowledge which is from richness of his personal experiences.

2. **Mentor** tells his followers the stories of his success that is a fodder for inspiring and developing their skills, personality and character.

3. **Mentor** can assess follower's strengths and weaknesses and point out the areas where they need to do improvements.

4. **Mentor** gives moral backing and cheer leading support that gives hope for success and see the light at the end of the tunnel.

5. **Mentor** help to the followers to know their boundaries of success that they required to set for themselves.

6. **Mentor** is as like a GURU, who help the disciple by offering harsh advice to overcome defects. But at the same time he gently support from within like a potter.

7. **Mentor** helps us in setting for the measurable goals.

Whether in professional work or in spiritual growth, the results depend upon not just hard work, but also on smart work. This is where Mentor became valuable. We receive proper guidance from the Mentor. Good Mentors can save us from the countless mistakes, and the years of fumbling in the dark.

®®®

38. Developing Supervisory Skills

Every Leader, for his effective and efficient functioning need to develop a team of competent supervisors. He need to choose the supervisors amongst his followers especially the employees of middle management cadre.

The supervisor should possess capacity of supervising the works being done by other employees. He need to be developed for making the best use of the resources with the help of employees so as to achieve best results for the organization. He should be the able person to interprets and pass on the messages to his subordinates that he received from the management.

A person who is supposed to supervise the work of other employees need to possess or should develop his skills in the areas such as: (i) managing change,

(ii) communication (iii) solving grievances of the employees, (iv) Time management, (v) facilating on the job training and (vi) Managing employee discipline.

Amongst the various duties of a supervisor, managing employee discipline at shop floor is a very important task the supervisor needs to carry out in his functioning. For an effective role in managing discipline at shop floor a supervisor, need to observe the following guidelines:

- Discipline is to be maintained on basis of a written set of rules, principles of natural justice and by observing the Laws applicable.
- Disciplinary action against an erring employee should be recommended only after knowing the circumstances and on basis of the relevant facts.
- In process of disciplinary action, the Supervisor should not threaten to the employee or argue with his or be angry with such employee who committed the misconduct.

- If an employee is doing well or his performance is found poor, then such employee should be told about the same immediately.

TRAINING & DEVELOPMENT:

Leader should take initiative for providing necessary training to the supervisors working with him. Training programme need to be a well-planned, structured and designed activity on basis of the job study.

Training should be after taking following steps viz.

1. After telling training needs to the employees, get them ready for attending to the training programme.

2. During the training programme, explain to the employee as to haw a job to be performed.

3. Employees to be informed about when they do their job rightly and wrongly.

4. Leader need to stand nearby to the employee when he does the work. Employee right kind of training needs can be identified after observing his working activity.

@@@

About the Author

Mohan Raghunath Khanvilkar was born in June 1951 in the village Nerle of Sindhudurg District. He completed his primary and secondary education in the village and after S.S.C. exam. came to Mumbai city in search of employment and higher education. He joined the Government of India service in the year 1971. Thereafter he joined Morning College and started further education. He completed graduation in Economics subject of Art studies and LL B degree from the University of Mumbai in the year-1983. Thereafter, he did a post-graduate Diploma in Personnel Management & Industrial Relations from Bharatiya Vidhya Bhavan Mumbai. He also completed a postgraduate Master Degree in Personnel Management from University of Pune, with First Class. He left Government of India service in July. 1983 and joined employment in a public limited company i.e. Narmada Cement Co. Ltd. in Mumbai. He continued his services in the Human Resources Departments of about seven different organizations and retired in March 2011 after completing forty-one years of his total services. He has written many articles, books and conducted many lectures for the students of management institutions in Mumbai. Presently he is as an Advisor to various organizations in Mumbai.

ଛଛଛ

SUPPLEMENTARY READING

1. Norman Vincent Peal – The Power of positive thinking - Om Books International.

2. Swami Mukundananda – The Science of Mind Management – West land Publications Pvt. Ltd.,

3. Ken Shelton, Editor – PERSONAL EXCELLENCE. – Jaico Publishing House.

4. Harvard Business Review, Boston, Massachusetts - LEADERSHIP.

5. **J.R.D. TATA** - The Magic of Leadership By – CYRUS M. GONDA.

6. Swami Mukundananda "7 Divine Laws To Awaken Your Best Self" Harper Collins Publishers India.

7. Dr. Ram Kulkarni - Personality Development. – Pratik Prakashan – Nasik.

8. Wonder House – World's Greatest Leaders.

9. Pranay - SWAMI VIVEKANANDA - Spirituality for Leadership & Success.

10. Ted Nicholas – Secrets of Entrepreneurial Leadership.- Forward By - Joseph Sugarman

11. The complete book of YOGA BY: Swami Vivekananda.

@@@

www.ingramcontent.com/pod-product-compliance
Lightning Source LLC
LaVergne TN
LVHW091050150826
845673LV00002B/535
* 9 7 9 8 8 9 6 7 3 8 4 0 4 *